South Jersey Sand

A Memoir in Poetry

South Jersey Sand

A Memoir in Poetry by

Jean Anne Feldeisen

© 2026 Jean Anne Feldeisen. All rights reserved.
This material may not be reproduced in any form, published,
reprinted, recorded, performed, broadcast,
rewritten or redistributed without
the explicit permission of Jean Anne Feldeisen.
All such actions are strictly prohibited by law.

Cover design by Shay Culligan
Cover image by Lena Polishko on Unsplash
Author photo by Kimberly Reed

ISBN: 978-1-63980-840-3
Library of Congress Control Number: 2025951560

Kelsay Books
502 South 1040 East, A-119
American Fork, Utah 84003
Kelsaybooks.com

One of this book's stories is about my family.
I wish to dedicate the poems of *South Jersey Sand*
to the next generations.

With all my love to Cara, Len, Andrew, Emily,
Megan, Cheyenne, Sarah, Brandon, Lindsey, Jordan,
and our new great-granddaughter, Meabh.

As always, my love and deepest respect
for my husband and best friend, Don.

Acknowledgments

Versions of the following poems first appeared in various literary publications, sometimes with different titles, and I want to thank the editors for bringing them into the world:

Bracken: "New Jersey Pine Barrens" (nominated for Best of the Net)
Comstock Review, Muriel Craft Bailey Contest 2024: "No need" (Finalist)
Eunoia Review: "Flamingo"
Fairy Tale Magazine: "I Worry That My Grandchildren . . ."
The Hopper: "A Chance to Spring"
The MacGuffin: "Love at Seventy-Five"
The Midcoast Villager: "Generational"
Mockingheart Review: "1913: The Yukon"
Neologism Poetry Journal: "Blue Sting: a Ghazal," "Strange Birds"
Not All Are Weeping (Main Street Rag, 2023): "Atlantic City, NJ: 1920," "Visiting Uncle Murray in the Senior Facility," "a small paradigm shift," "How to build a burger," "Final Listening," "The blinds are shut," "The tent party," "I just want to see her face"
The Orchards Poetry Journal: "Cold"
The Raven's Perch: "Jersey Devil," "Workshop Attic," "Touring King Tut"
Rising Phoenix Review: "my brother runs down"
Spank the Carp: "The Marriage House"
Thimble Literary Magazine: "A Manor of Endings," "At the edge"
The Turning Leaf Journal: "Jab, Jab, Cross," "Road Trip," "to change directions"
Vita Poetica: "Unrouted"

Special Thanks

My deepest admiration and appreciation goes to my teacher and mentor Brian Evans-Jones for his intelligence, creativity and kindness along with an ability to give respectful but unfailingly honest feedback about my poetry. His invaluable leadership with the Poetry Parlor group has given me the tools and encouragement I needed to work seriously at my writing. I am grateful to all the members of the Poetry Parlor, past and present, for inspiring and encouraging me. Thanks to the original members of Gibbs Library Writing Group: especially Dorothy Hopkins, Peg Hobbs, Chris DeGroff, and Karen Jelenfy, who labored with me over some of these poems. Special thanks to my poet friends and readers, Terry Karnan, Nancy Wheaton, Beth Fox and Lauren Vermette.

Contents

South Jersey Sand   15
Road Trip   16

I. Earlier . . .

Philadelphia, PA: 1907   25
The Yukon: 1913   26
Atlantic City, NJ: 1920   28
Pleasantville, NJ: 1929   29
A Single Egg   31

II. and then . . .

Edge   35
Ghazal: Blue Sting   36
Safe Place   38
Homage to Dad's Christmas Tree   40
Flamingo   42
Que Sera: Doris Day, 1956   44
Dressed Up   45
Unrouted   46
Jersey Devil   49
Workshop Attic   50
Touring King Tut   52
Strange Birds   54
Barrier Beach   55
Little Beach   56
Adapting   58

III. and so . . .

New Jersey Pine Barrens	63
Jab Jab Cross	64
At the Edge	67
Where's Linda?	68
Sugar: A Villanelle	70
The Marriage House	71
New Jersey Beach Sand	74

IV. after that . . .

My Mother Is Having Her Ninety-Fifth Birthday	77
Pink Suit	78
Visiting Uncle Murray in the Senior Facility	80
Her Son	83
A Small Paradigm Shift	85
How to Build a Burger	86
Dementia Framed	88
Cold	90
A Manor of Endings	92
One Woman's Breath	94
Cuttings	96
My Brother Runs Down	97
Final Listening	99
No Need	100

V. Goodbye . . .

The Blinds Are Shut	105
Dragging My Feet	107
The Tent Party	108
I Just Want to See Her Face	110
Birdwing	111

VI. and now . . .   113

A Chance to Spring	115
I Worry That My Grandchildren . . .	117
Best Behavior	119
Love at Seventy-Five	120
After the Death Certificate	121
Generational	124
To Change Direction	126

South Jersey Sand

I take the big metal spoon, twist it in the dirt, let the wrist's
momentum toss quartz and granite into air. Fossils of shells and
long dead creatures mix with bits of root and glass. They scatter,
some fall back in.

Dig deeper. Maybe find gold or silver, a few coins, pennies even?
See a metal gleam
at the edge of the hole. What is it? A tomb for a pet mouse?
Silver box with a lock of baby hair?

Deeper. I dig up tiny shoes, marbles, silver spoons, all that's left
of childhood—
once-colorful cookie tins now dented, rusted, full of sand.

What do I really want? Scribbled notes from lovers, a hole
scissoring a face from a sepia portrait, a deathbed apology? Can I
guess from a sober face or fancy speech misdeeds swept into
the compost heap?

You reap whatever turns up, isn't that how it goes? My lifetime
spent gleaning missed clues from picked-over digs. I sift out
unnecessary words. Fill the wheel barrow. Tip it onto a page.

Road Trip

*When you drive, the road goes under the car and comes
out the back,* my Grandson once said—so observant
of the mechanics of things, and how we appear to sit still

in the seats but nevertheless move forward. I huddle
under a blanket and shift in the front seat, clutch
my coffee. That's my goal, move forward.

My husband drives, glides us onto the highway
jostles into a queue of cars and trucks, the road sliding
under all of us and already I question my plan

to go back, the five hundred miles from Maine
to South Jersey. Hard to move on after the endings—
the funerals, cleaning, memories in the dumpster,

jolt of the slammed door. Going forward or backward
the sharp thorns of memory snag you,
create an uncomfortable prickle of flesh.

***

Countless times we've taken this trip back, watched
the same reel of trees, rivers, mountains, sighed
over the impossible number of trucks and cars.

I know the kind of moving forward we'll find
when we arrive. My husband and I grew up in the country,
around a corner from each other, bicycled over back roads.

When we last saw our old home—a glut of Dunkin' Donuts,
McDonalds, and strip malls. Some familiar houses still stand,
flanked by new McMansions. New houses were built

where we played in the woods. Barrier beaches meant
to protect the mainland are a clutter of hotels and casinos.
All slammed against the water. Tourists who flock

to the shore make havoc of habitat of birds, deer,
sea creatures and human residents, as well. Now
it's hard to see the ocean, to find any wild places.

***

Hours later we enter New Jersey while I tick
off memories, some funny, some prickly. Merging
onto the Garden State Parkway, I remember its opening:

how proud we were of our fancy new roadway.
Awed by the men in the little toll booths
we kids fought to reach out dad's window,

hand him our quarter. *You look good
in your uniform,* my little brother yelled.
Past northern exits crowded with cars, then

over the Raritan River south, through the Pine Barrens—
mile after mile of dusty stunted trees. Heading
for exit 48 at the marshes near Chestnut Neck,

we wind a tight curve off the ramp to waving stalks
of Phragmites. At last. A deep sniff—rotten eggs,
the smell that so delighted my river-birthed mother.

***

Who knows what led my orphaned grandmother
from Philadelphia, my grandfather just home from the Yukon
to migrate and meet in a hotel in Atlantic City?

He was a cook, she a waitress twenty years younger.
My father's family began there. Mom's family'd been
here forever, Baymen tonging oysters and clams.

How fortunate I found a man who loved the water.
He fit well with the silent, tough, and hard working
watermen, my mother's kin. I admired that he returned

to the bay after college in Philadelphia, passing up
career opportunities, though he drew criticism
from family about finding *a real job*. His grandfather said,

You've gotta work with your head, boy, not your hands.
But, going back was right. He hated the city, begrudged
every minute away from the water, his boat and freedom.

***

Almost home now, we stop at the graveyard
where my mother's family has been buried
for generations. All the moving forward and backward

of their complex lives, along with what meaning
we squeeze from this, ends in stillness, under cold
slabs of stone, planted here and pained with names.

Mom and Dad close together. When my brother died at 20—
too soon to plan a grave—someone donated a small plot
so he'd be near family. What use are these markers? Yet,

last year we spent $1200 to buy a stone for my aunt
who didn't get one. After 74 years together, the couple
died in separate institutions, mislaid by each other.

Now Aunt Jean sits where she belongs,
next to Uncle Murray. Next to the rest of them.
My family—in dirt, remarked by stones.

***

The dirt here is called Downer Soil, a mixture
particular to South Jersey. After the last Ice Age
receding waters left behind a land of beach

with soil a large part sand, its water close to the surface.
Good for farming and forests, as long as you add plenty
of fertilizer and water to replace what leaches out easily.

We lived a mile from the back-bay, adjacent to a creek.
After a hard rain, as if an underground faucet was left open,
water rose up to cover the crabgrass in our lawn.

In summer we chased each other through these bogs.
Water covered our badminton field, left ankle-deep mud
under mom's clothesline. But we were Downer kids,

my brother, sister and I. We thrived here, our playground
a boggy mire of holes hidden by wet leaves,
bordered by bayberry and thick patches of briars.

***

The soil in our backyard was useless for growing things.
Mostly sand, it fell apart in your hands. We'd try to plant
a garden, turn up earth to drop tiny seeds, then keep watch

for roots beneath the cotyledons of radishes or zinnias.
Nothing. The seeds we planted never flourished. Only stunted
violets and dandelions pushed through the weeds in the lawn,

choked out by tougher things, things that belonged there,
like us. We picked flowers from neighbors' yards, sometimes
with permission, learned to stay quiet about arguments

at home. Didn't notice there was barely enough money
even when dad had a job. We ate Spam and Campbell's soup,
bread and butter, made ten-cent pitchers of Kool Aid.

Walked barefoot from the first day of school vacation
to the last. Tough as the soles of our feet, the briars we tamed,
the mud we stomped, the rude soil we tried to cultivate.

***

Stiff after the five-hundred-mile drive, I'm ready
to make the turn onto Brook Lane. My husband drives slowly
past the familiar house without turning in. I notice

the new owners have painted it red. Unfamiliar cars
park where I used to play. Everything seems wrong,
though I couldn't say what is missing. The house

itself looks cheerful, neat, and the yard landscaped.
Anyone would call it progress. We stop at the Little Brook.
I emerge from the car and try to pick out the entrance—

only a small patch of moss next to a feeble stream.
I peer between bamboo stalks which have invaded
the area, and look like prison bars.

The brook still smells of decaying vegetation
and festers memories—of fighting briars, playing
in the water, or hiding from craziness at home.

***

I could pretend it was someone else who used to live
here, with that family and that tree-swing and this sour
bit of brook, briar patch with no bamboo.

But I've come back to face the prickly memories. Up close,
I know something is different. Even the smell of the marshes
seems more poignant now, though it's probably not changed.

This trip, no mother with open arms and kisses.
No familiar room or bed to lay our cases.
No welcome at all. Only a Holiday Inn.

I remember a final visit—Mom pushed her walker,
a blue-flowered scarf on her head. How she sparkled,
I remember, and the sun that day was warm. She giggled

when we discovered a hidden patch of violets. I picked some
for her to put in a vase. We sat there, me on a low fence,
her in the walker, talked about I don't know what.

***

Mom is gone, but she would be happy
that we're here today. I consider my vast reservoir
of memories and pick a few special ones for a little vase.

Aren't our bodies always renewing? Scoured daily
cell by cell? The scab of the past soon separates
from virgin skin. I see through eyes that belong to another,

older, a woman who lives somewhere else. I think
my grandson was only partly right—when the road slides
under the car, what comes out the back is brand new.

I smile at my husband, remembering all we've passed,
climb back in my seat. We take another turn round the house
then drive off. I let myself be carried forward.

I. Earlier . . .

Philadelphia, PA: 1907

But the Saturday before
she held tight to his big hand.
They stopped to buy hot chestnuts from a cart.
How he bounced them hand to hand, making her giggle.
How one escaped—she chased it across the sidewalk.
They laughed as he cracked the nuts open
and they ate, burning fingers and lips.
That day he called her precious, smoothed
her long brown hair.

She watches by the tall window
a small black spider climb the drapery.
She has never been afraid of them, but today
she trembles.

Across the room
              stern gray heads nod toward her
                            and whisper.
The sun is blinding in her eyes,
            she's lost sight of the spider—
Ah, see it scramble up the wall . . .

. . . nothing else to do . . .   *Quakers will take her . . .*

They have chopped off her hair clear above the nape
—cloaked her in a long black dress.

She cries now, knowing her father
will feel wretched
about her hair.

The Yukon: 1913

> My grandfather Theodore G. Felsberg, Sr. was a prospector
> in Alaska and the Yukon, around the turn of the 19th century.

I was only fifteen, like you, then.
Now, I squat over a pitiful fire atop
twenty feet of frozen peat.
Clasp cold and frost-bit hands,
think about home, wonder
what to make of my own lies.
You want advice, lad?

I left New Jersey years ago lusting
for rumor of gold. One should forgive
a young man taking that bait, with full strength
and long years still before him.
The first time we found grains of gold
in the sheet steel pan, I saw my life
unfold as I'd planned it.
Going home respected, a rich man.

I threw myself into it, slogged
long trails by dogsled and foot,
built cabins, tended endless fires
to melt the peat, dug all winter,
winched dirt up in buckets.
Always testing the pan, hoping
to find the vein.

In my twenty years there've been
many rock-hard lessons about men and cold
but no gold.
None panned out.

I crouch here, oddly familiar
with the rank sweat of fear, the bitter taste
of lost dreams and lost mates—
all drowned in drifts of riches.

Don't be snared by fancy stories, lad.
Like a leg-hold trap, they clamp tight.
An animal will gnaw off a leg to get free.

Atlantic City, NJ: 1920

We walked the Boardwalk that night.
Her long brown hair stretched past her waist,
blew around us—her smile, her delight
in my stories, blurred my eyes.

I bought salt water taffy, pop and hot dogs
for us to share. The wind's salt smell,
pound of dark waves on the beach,
rushed my asking, *Might I kiss you?*

I had wandered east, abandoned
a lifetime prospecting gold in Alaska
This woman—barely twenty,
myself nearly forty. After
the ice-cold dangers I was pulled to her
like frozen hands to a fire.

She ended up in my bed, me with a vigor
I barely remembered, salt water taffy
tangled in her hair, and smiling.
Smiling at me. Of course we would marry.

We had a simple service.
After all those long years—wed
to the forsaken and unknown of trail life,
I claim a constant wife.

Pleasantville, NJ: 1929

> Before the stock market crash, my grandfather,
> Theodore G. Felsberg, Sr., owned a lunch car, *Ted's Lunch*.

Three in the afternoon, Susanna worries
the soup with a metal spoon, shifts
the fussing Arthur on her hip.
The baby grabs at the pot lid making it fall
to the linoleum floor with a crash!

Her ears ring and radio hums with talk
of something wrong with the money.
She fiddles with the baby's ringlets. Why isn't he back?
Swats the tiny hand away from the stove again,
plunks him on the floor near his brother, Teddy.
He went to the bank before lunchtime,
been gone for hours, what's keeping him?

She paces the kitchen, brown braid swinging fierce,
Teddy has outgrown his new shoes already.
She needs yard goods to sew the dress Cora begs
for a birthday party. She already owes the grocer
for last month. How will they pay?

Teddy whines for the third time *When
will Daddy come home?* She cringes, stoops
to smooth the boy's head with her hand.
Soon. I'm sure he'll be here soon.

When, at last, the door creaks open he stands,
steadies himself on the frame. The boys

turn to their father. Susanna snags
her husband's fear-wide eyes, smiles
to embrace whatever he will say.

A Single Egg

Imagine a world where your daily chore was
to carry one egg a half mile on your bicycle
to the home of a little girl with polio
who needed a fresh egg.

Imagine this child desperate for the nourishment
from a single egg. Perhaps the family
had no eggs and not enough food

so that one egg would make a difference. And
imagine the family who could spare just one a day.
In that family, every day, perhaps, someone went without.

I guess it must have been a fresh egg
since no one, in 1934, had refrigeration.
My father would have been about nine—

Old enough to be given this task, but
not so old he was scornful of the family's obligation
to the girl, still proud of his contribution.

(I keep imagining he carried the egg on a spoon,
but I suppose I am scrambling that up with an egg race)

Picture him—a single egg in his shirt pocket,
up on the pedals, stiff arms on the handlebars,
with determined eyes, carefully pumping up and down.

II. and then . . .

Edge

The Little Brook was ours. It abutted our back yard with a swampy edge, so we walked down the road to enter. Our inventions—leaves, sticks, paper—added to the water, were caught up by the current and off they went. We had tiny reasons for what we tossed in. Mostly tests. To see if our craft would float. Or survive the dark unknown of the tunnel under the road. Could we run as fast? And how far? Would it get caught in a dam of fallen branches? Or break away to be carried all the way, we imagined, to the bay?

We dangled feet where sand was warm from the sun. Lingered where water striders skated the surface, and frogs landed in eddies. Wormed our toes into mud littered with torn and decaying sticks and leaves, knew to avoid jagged edges of glass bottles and tin cans thrown from car windows.

When I grew older, a safe place to hide. To soak my asphalt-heated soles in icy water. A mossy seat for dreaming, peaceful with babble and warbling birds. Then to go home—not so pretty, and not always safe. To face the battered cans of family and our father's jagged edge.

Ghazal: Blue Sting

I'm three, outside in the sandbox. I wriggle rounded lumps of arms
    and legs into sand
to see the sky parade its cloud shapes. Gaze up, watching blue.

I craved a blue the soft of butterfly wings and a partly clouded sky.
Off Brigantine beach the blue sea stretched to Europe, the blue sky
    to heaven. Floating blue.

A month before my birth my grandfather died, a perpetually
    unreachable prize.
I spent years imagining his eyes as Grandmom described: *the most
    dazzling blue.*

Jealous as mother slips my new sister into the palest blue flannel
    sacque,
A paler silk ribbon threads the bottom to contain tiny feet that
    wildly fling blue.

One Christmas my fair-haired sister wears a golden ballerina
    costume,
a shiny tiara, transforms into a princess. That year, Grandmom
    made twin blue

and red dresses. I knew the sky blue one was for me. But, *you
are better suited to red,* she said. The princess wins blue.

Safe Place

The workshop smelled of wood and paint.
Turpentine and dirt. He made it first—
a place to hold his tools, keep things dry
while he built the new house.

Evenings after work he'd hoist me up
to sit on the long workbench. Safe
from sharp blades and hot stove,
I'd swing my legs, watch him work.

I'd ask questions, play with baby food jars
of nails and screws. Beg him to show me
boxing moves with the leather punching bag
that hung from a hook in the ceiling.

In the middle of it all, a pot-bellied cast iron stove.
He taught me to fill it without being burned.
To lift the knobbed handle, swing the door open—
stand back—throw a small stick into the fire.

I watched him make a cut with the hand saw
after careful measurement with a folding ruler
to the short black checkmark
from the thick pencil behind his ear.

He'd smooth a rough plank with wooden plane,
make sweet smelling curls I loved
to gather and twist around my fingers, dangle
from my hair like Shirley Temple's ringlets.

He could make anything. Choose a nail
from a jar. Hammer boards together
whack, whack. Sawhorses.
A new stepstool. Neat bed for a doll.

I was three when he finished the roof.
Mom took my picture, standing proud.
One foot on each side of the ridge board,
touching the sky with Dad.

Homage to Dad's Christmas Tree

For the scraggly spruce tree Dad chopped down
in the woods and set against the back of the house
until Christmas Eve. For the smell of the sapwood,
the scratch of its branches as we brushed past.
How we ignored the few browning needles,
the huge gaps between some of the branches
but turned and turned it, to help
the tree show its best side.

For the night before Christmas when excitement
fizzed in us kids like bubbles
in the Coca Cola we drank from slender green bottles.
How Dad set up the tree and strung lights
around and around in brilliant swirls
and how we three hopped and popped
ready to explode, wanting to help.
Jostled and argued to get closer to him
place our favorite ornaments
until he lost his temper and shouted at us
to shut up. For Mom who stepped in
helped us add the tinsel, lured us to our beds
Santa mustn't find you still awake.

For how we believed in him
and tolerated the ruse,
even when we got to be ten or twelve,
because we wanted to hear
from behind our closed doors
the sound of Dad's feet stamping,
his excited voice hollering,
as he listens to the reindeer on the roof,
their harness bells ringing,
Merry Christmas Santa,
Stomp, Stomp, Jingle, Jingle.
He's gone, kids, you can come in now.

Flamingo

The new owners have painted my old house a cheery red
that reminds me of the flamingo wall dad insisted on,
flamboyant in those years when he first started
to make money enough to have choices.
Perhaps a memory from the Navy
of bright painted houses on the cliffs of Gibraltar.
Or the birds we spied on vacations to Florida,
standing in bunches on tall stems.

One long bright red-pink
wall in the living room, a stunner,
the others white. Hard to match
with second hand furniture, clutter of three kids
and a wife devoid of decoration.

It was his castle, built of a man's
determination to rise to the need of his
growing family, meet the expectations of all
the well-to-do ancestors and in-laws.
The little house his rising—his craft, his connections,
and the leftovers—cabinets, tiles, paint—
from other buildings he'd worked on.

Sitting at our kitchen table, I watched
as he drew lines with his pencil,
connected little squares, to signify bigger rooms
that he said would soon—
like magic—appear outside.

I helped in the way of a four-year-old, fetched
tools, brought coffee in a thermos, asked
endless questions. Learned needle-nose pliers
from Phillips screwdrivers from the big red-handled
channel locks, watched as he poured footings,
laid blocks, layered on lumber.

I can still smell the sawn boards, the sawdust,
the damp under the house where my sister
and I played hide and seek, built doll houses
or pens for box turtles from the cut ends
of two by fours.

Perhaps the house remembers, too. Helps tint
the faded aqua of its toxic asbestos siding
the color of a young man's dreams.

Que Sera: Doris Day, 1956

Mom always hummed it
when she washed dishes
used it for comfort, though
I wonder how much of it she bought.

More likely felt a welcome reprieve
just to stand in one place for a time
hands circling on their own
like driving a familiar road home.

Did she stand humming at the sink
that day, after Dad shattered every precious
flowered dish of her grandmother's
against the refrigerator? *What will be will be?*

Or did she reach some limit of what
a young woman could spare—
three babies, up to both elbows
in the hot water?

Wary the next time he threatened, she threw
the heavy ashtray to chip on his elbow
marched herself down the road where
she could catch the bus for home.
Que sera, sera.

Dressed Up

Mom gave me a dime to iron
each cotton shirt my father wore to work.
Wet it with a sprinkler—an old coke bottle
with perforated rubber stopper—
roll it up to soak. Then, with slap of hot
steel, press stiff collar and cuffs, flatten
the rectangular yoke to shape it.

I disliked ironing sleeves, rounded,
and a devil to unwrinkle. Did them next,
then slid the point of the iron
between buttons on the front,
then over the flat buttonhole side.

Finally free to breeze across
the expanse of his full back,
point the darts carefully. Finished.
Then ease onto a hanger and fasten
the top button. My father made decent again.

Unrouted

Once, when religion meant goodness,
my family sat all together
in a pew near the front on the left, sat
upright, and quiet, if not always reverent.

My sister and I wedged between Mom and Dad,
little brother contained under Dad's arm.
My sister's straight blond hair swung in my face
when we whispered together. Sunlight routed

through reds and blues of stained glass, loud
organ music vibrated in my belly. There was reading.
Reciting and repeating. Dad's bold tenor
poured out familiar hymns. This interminable

sitting still the start of every Sunday of our lives.
We older girls listen, scramble to understand
the big words—Salvation, Sacrifice,
God's Love for His People. One thing we understand:

we in this pew *are* God's people. They hand out
our values along with gold pins and white Bibles. Our
places assured as we take our seats and profess to
believe the words we recite.

And we believe that God loves us and forgives us,
even me who just yesterday stole a velvety bite of Dad's
Hershey Bar from his forbidden top bureau drawer.
Even my sister who kicks the baby under the table
to make him cry.

***

As a child it was fed to me
—a nourishing gruel—
I swallowed it whole

*How did God become Jesus and how
did he walk on water*
                        and then he was
crucified but got up again
                (like boxers
who you think are down but stumble
to their feet
                not done with you yet)

Teachers smoothed
incomplete knowledge
with a basting of greasy faith
        its slippery consistency
covering multitudes

When I dumped the bowl
in the compost bin
what took root?

***
                        Didn't they tell you?
while
you stomped
with the other kids
to the steady beat
of On   ward
Christ   ian
Sold   iers

March   ing
As to   (both excuse and reason for) War
repetitive rhythm   drilled into the
body a blind   obedience
to your Captain   no matter the cost?

                               Didn't they tell you?
                               All
that soldiers   killed

or what trust   priests might betray
in the robes   of gods?

***

Traitor, I whisper to myself.
Ashamed, even as I speak
the words, like Judas,
            I never knew it.

For I miss the organ swelling,
the brilliant light,
sitting rooted
to the same seat
every week.

Knowing
exactly what I must do
to be saved.

Jersey Devil

Stories of unearthly screams
in the woods next the marshes of Leeds Point.
Little devil child sprung full-armor,
you thirteenth child of a mother
who could not save or name you.
What rumor invented the cloven hooves
that held you upright? The horns,
the bat-like wings, the soul-black eyes?
They say you flew off into thick of briars
across the marshes to the creek
with anguished cries sometime after midnight.
While she stood silent, trembling,
her moist eyes trying to pierce the mist
out the window where you'd flown.

Your cries forever shiver those souls
who stray too near the old brick house.

Workshop Attic

A ladder of two by fours nailed between studs
made it possible to ascend to the low attic
where we would crawl, on the lookout for wasps,
heads tucked tight against nails.

There we found odd cast offs
from our parents' mysterious childhoods:
old magazines and baby beds,
picture frames with portraits of unknown people
Dad's Navy trunk we weren't to open.

A strange black spinning thing intrigued us:
fitted with slots
for dozens of red and black poker chips.
We'd spin then dump them,
stack in piles of red and black,
then, again, fill and spin and stack.

We open the hinged window,
                    let it flap
against its chain, then stretched
            way out   over open
                                          air
to reach the sassafras tree, pull off
a twig to chew.

On rainy days
    our attic was Dad's navy vessel,
the rain slamming her
  against hurricane-high
    waves in '44.

Once in a while Dad himself would poke his head
above the floor, to make sure we were okay,
  to remember forgotten play.

Touring King Tut

> 1976: the King Tut Exhibit came to The Metropolitan
> Museum of Art in New York City

Two hours through endless dusty trees
my sister and I read and reread
the museum brochure
our legs stuck to the seat
of Uncle Murray's Volkswagen bug
hot even with windows cranked down.
Finally—through the Lincoln Tunnel
straight up to the Met.

We enter fifteen minutes apart
One at a time—

      Taking pictures, touching,
                   even   breathing on
the ancient relics   forbidden.

   I am a blank slate.
Vow to remember every scene.
      Sniff the scent   the muted sounds
  air entombed   thousands of years ago
           the red of burnished pottery
  that stored water for gods to drink.

I imagine the feel on my fingers
            the metallic taste against teeth
of jewel-encrusted   rings necklaces anklets.
     Savor the soft sheen of aged gold
           lining eating utensils

encrusted on clothes.   Everywhere
            the gleam
    of emeralds rubies   diamonds.

    In me   a frisson of miracle.
            This first time—like a first kiss—
    no expectations
no memories summon disappointments
                    to drop
            like discarded tickets on the sidewalk.
Instead, I straighten to balance on my head
                each impossibly tall headdress.

    And, after,
shabby Sixth Street crowded with cars.
Uncle Murray treats us to dinner
a Chinese below-the-street restaurant.
I can't taste it.
        My teeth still chew
                on gems
lifted to my mouth with golden sticks.

Strange Birds

As kids we spelled it like we thought
a crow's call would be spelled. A-U-K, Auk.
Hollered it loud to talk, to find each other
in the woods, or a strange place: *Auk, Auk.*

Never mind, years later, we realize
our word named a large Arctic bird
long-extinct. When I hear the call
I look up, hunt for my siblings.

Meeting my sister for lunch yesterday
I saw her pop her head in the restaurant door,
scan the room. Without thought—
out of my mouth flew a loud *Auk, Auk.*

The heads of those at the next tables
turned to stare in unison. I quickly looked
bored. Had someone screamed like a bird?
Giving me away, she homed in neatly on our nest.

Barrier Beach

This barrier raises
no gate to block the road
no road   only shifting sand.

Bemused by wind and tide
contracts, expands,
holds   breathing space
for the mainland.

Little Beach

> The last uninhabited barrier island on the Atlantic coast
> off of Atlantic County, New Jersey

Locals say it barely exists these days,
but I see it clearly. Though mostly I remember

him. Tanned-brown arms, hairs bleached golden
grazing my breasts as he helps me out of the boat.
Surf pounding on the shore. We two alone on the dunes.

A fox runs off, her kits tumbling over each other.
Seagulls and Terns wheel above, Plovers and Spots
hunt flat-footed at the edge of the surf.

An abandoned cabin he said was called Red's
though there's no evidence of Red. Instead,
screens with holes big enough for raccoons.

He told me of high tides that flooded the marshes.
How they drove the boat fast to get here, once
when he, Brother Bob, Cousin Bruce, camped out all night.

We cook hotdogs over a fire he built, I marvel
he can carry it all, in his boat, in his arms.
A blanket, wood, food, me.
At eighteen—enough for us both.
The island no barrier.

Adapting

                    Ragged
                        edge
                              of ocean
                                        pulses
                          pushes
                              waves of sand further

                                                  out
                            sea   levels rise
                                  temperature

                                      changes Ghost
                            crabs   Hermit crabs,
                    Whelks   Periwinkles dig deep
                                          in sand
Dented blue cooler
        clinks beer
                ice cream truck
    sings past
        giant umbrellas land
  beach towels

      brief suits flatter
          bodies laid
              flat on sand
Dune buggies   smooth out
     footprints
erase   natural dunes
                      BEACHES DISAPPEARING
          interference
              with habitat required

                    Piping Plover makes   shallow
                            scrapes
                                        in   fragile dunes
                                    sheltering
                    grasses
                                    near Terns,   Common
                                                and Least
                        What happens
                    to living things   in sand ?

BEACH REPLENISHMENT

Dredges
     Pump   offshore
         sand bars   Soon
 beach reappears.
Let life guard   flags fly
              jingling ice cream
            truck
                music
    sun   bathers
children dig   near surf
                      What happens between
                there   and here ?
           Next
              year
               fewer   plovers
                        terns

             periwinkles   crabs whelks
     Dead   jangle
          of   shells
                      in sand

III. and so . . .

New Jersey Pine Barrens

In Memoriam: M. A. F. (1966–1987)

The largest contiguous forest on the Eastern Seaboard
between Maine and the Florida Everglades.

Sixteen, you say you'll be a Piney. Live alone in a crude hut,
hunt squirrel and possum, spit your tobacco. Sure,
you could lose a lot of sins in a million acres
of ugly Pygmy Pines. The Barrens are hot as hell,
dry as sun-bleached bone, yet underneath, a prize—
enough aquifer water for the entire state. You, too, brim
with untapped springs, but want to hide here,
follow the deer trails, kick up dust that settles
as gray slime on perspiring skin while hundreds
of chiggers crawl up your legs, burrow in. Nice—
a lingering itch to remind you of your swim
at a hole in the woods on Oswego River.
You grab onto a rope, swing out, drop deep
into the icy dark of iron-red water. Lucky

I was there that time you couldn't swim, brother,
snatched your hair as you went down, pulled you safe.

Jab Jab Cross

She watched her father closely while he swung
his big hammer to hit the nail head on.
Sat on the workbench, kicked her legs,
followed strong arms as he let fly combinations,
practiced counters, called them out *Jab, jab, cross,*
Jab, cross, left as he pummeled
the punching bag hung from the ceiling.
Friday nights they saw the boxing matches
on TV together. She sang all the commercials

but eyed him like you would a snake,
prepared to leap clear. Learned
to smile and take his arm at the right
moment, carry his lunchbox and skip (gaily).

She hustled arguing brother and sister
to another room, picked up stray toys in his way.
Knew his anger came fast and left fast.
Knew they'd be safe if they could get   out of range. Knew
because, sometimes, it happened to her, too.
A hot blur of rage—*I hate you*—followed by shame.
      Like her he was sorry afterwards.

***

A new mother, she stared her father in the eye
    Never dare hit my daughter,
        even if
            she deserves it.

***

The day the child came home early from play
with the neighbor boy, confessed to riding on his older
brother's motorbike,
something about Playboy magazines
      maybe worse details that
           the mother didn't—really—hear
because rage struck
      shook loose guilt (*How could you let this happen?*)
  and fear.
She screamed at her daughter
without thought
grabbed a coffee can and
    slammed
          the blame onto the child.

***

Imagine you were ten. Singled out
by this older boy. You really just wanted to play
with Legos or feed the swayback horse in the field.
        Awed to be taken for a ride on his bike but
    confused by his touch.

You think it is safe to tell your mother.
    But she just goes crazy.
No, you are alone.

You suspect
      silence is safer.
How do you feel?
Did you have fun at the party?
What did you learn in school?

Fine. No. Nothing. With each *No*
         slam the door between you.

***

The hurled can laid
              a path—to let fly
     coffee cups, wine glasses, a fork
across a party,   a slip
       off the dock into dark water,
  open the door of the car
            moving.   Open
    to whatever tumbled out.

***

For years you've worn
        the family shame
            to rags.
   You ache   to return
            the can to the shelf
               the fork to your hand.

Still, if you can dodge the punch
       thrown   into the next generation—
counter
         in the shape of a pause.

At the Edge

I'm waiting for the locomotive and its chain
of clacking boxcars and caboose to roar
around the corner of Daddy's train board.
Electric smell of friction
and the building fury
of the train as I sit,
as close to the edge
as I dare, pray
it will make the turn but knowing
it sometimes derails *right here*
in a spectacular screech,
rims sparking metal.
I tie my eyes to the track,
my face nearly touching
as long as I can stand
before it is coming—
too close,
a scream escapes—
I pull back,
safe.

Since then, my sentence
to wait at the edge of dread.

Where's Linda?

Above roar of diesel engine, squeal of brakes,
voices of twenty-some unruly kids
I make out her name
a shadowy story
of the window they crawled from
sister brother mother gone
my friend burned
over 97% of her fourteen-year body.

I heard *Still alive.*

The bus roars past the school
up to the ruined house,
smoke still rising.
Mr. Ramsey opens the door
for me.

In the familiar yard I freeze
not just from February cold.
Sink to the ground.
Stare at what were windows,
now burned holes
like half-closed eyes in the wall.
Roof collapsed,
charred smell in the air.

Wisps of three—spirits, I suppose—
        only three
circle the smoking yard, round and round
near wooden slats of toddler swing,
new blue Christmas bike, the mother
around her babies.

I sit alone, watch them swirl or hover
whatever ghosts do, wailing.
I breathe in the seared air
waiting for her.
        Still only three.

I cling to a 3% wisp of hope.

Sugar: A Villanelle

I just had to taste that shiny sweet so I tried
to crawl to the cut-glass candy dish. Daddy smacked me.
I craved what was forbidden. Unsatisfied,

I grew a powerful need for what was denied,
filled pockets with candies—pink, yellow and green
I just had to taste that sweetness. I tried

to steal a plump tangerine from another kid; she cried
but I didn't confess. I'd never be so mean.
In spite of it, the craving wasn't satisfied.

Took coconut eggs from the teacher's closet, lied.
Class profits from the candy sale—I stuffed and ate.
Wanted to devour that pastel sweetness, then denied

I'd done it. Filled pockets, shopping bags. Stirred up
bowls of brown sugar and butter, a secret treat,
but, my craving was never satisfied.

I plied all the vices: I'd lie, cheat, steal, but defied
you to say I wasn't the nicest girl you could meet.
I needed that shiny sweetness and I tried.
Decades later—still craving—still unsatisfied.

The Marriage House

       A boy in a red cap rides his bike to the baseball field
               flips
                        upside down
     for the girl who has answers to all the questions in
chemistry class.

                They marry and ride home with a
       string of trout caught at Uncle Gus's pond   hanging
downside up like flags from   the back of the bike,
     to build a house together.

       He brings white pine trees, cozies up to a local watering
hole,
             rides a clever motorized bicycle
                       (which he pedals furiously
when a car goes by).
             She contributes a bright green
                              and bitter lime
marmalade,
                her grandmother's silverware,
                and the   sure path to salvation.

They both hammer and nail the thing together
       He fusses about construction,   she slap
               dashes everything,   but the   upside
    is
               they start building.

His beaten up stuffed donkey,   her London Fog raincoat,
  his clam-shaped boat,   her Steinway
              grand persona
his mother's perfect chicken

            her father's terrifying
               judgments.

    For the downside of lumber they use
     his lies,
       her violence,
 his avoidance,   her arrogance. Reload
the secret fears
     they vomit up at night
       for nails.

The house grows. No one   notices
    as termites tear their way   up
   from the worried foundation, casually chew through

     coffee cups thrown,   decisions smashed.

  Boxed up feelings
        in wine glasses and butter dishes
         stashed away for future use.

       Holes turn into
              caverns and   unsure   floors,

                  lower levels eaten into
                  l   a   c   e.

                One day walking   up   the steps
            she plunges through rotten cotton batting and dead
bugs,

    falls
        down

                into an unexpected
                cavity filled
                      with his steeled feelings and pretend
promises.
        He finds a place
                          at the other end of the
basement
    with her abandoned playthings—desires, plans,
sincerities wrapped up in   little boxes with bright paper.
       They ask   what else is hidden here?

New Jersey Beach Sand

The New Jersey coast is the landward boundary of the Atlantic continental shelf. Beaches along the coast are composed primarily of unconsolidated tourists who disagree over parking spaces, the right to build castles on the sand, or erect giant umbrellas. The silt was left behind by glaciers compacting a jumble of crumpled McDonalds wrappers, smashed fries and pink wads of bubble gum as well as gravel carried in their shoes from as far away as Pennsylvania and New York. These visitors were eroded and pounded fine from streams of harried mothers toting cars full of kids to the shore while Dad stays in the city for work until Friday night when he joins the coastal plain sediments, building over the past 125,000 years, all lining the parkway and expressway heading for the beach.

The sediment is directly exposed to wave action from the influx of visitors flowing down these pathways. The eroded material from the headlands is reworked by waves and incorporated into imaginative visions of politicians, shuttled into place by gulls charged with sediment transport.

The composition of tourists varies slightly by location, with northern beaches containing more Jewish businesspeople from New York and southern locations more Italian families from Philadelphia, for example. There is very little difference in coloration of the population; most tan to a dark brown eventually.

IV. after that . . .

My Mother Is Having Her Ninety-Fifth Birthday

and I start worrying over writing—will my words make
              something matter—as a crow
       flies over plum trees their white blossoms

wave and one might infer thousands
              of tiny flying creatures circling
       to pollinate other trees—   I wonder that NASA

decides to study an asteroid—sends a probe
              to its very surface   some say it will be hotter
    out west while in the northeast we become colder

and I long for the chill clarity of a hot
             cup of coffee to still my
   buzzing—   this simmering

sphere and here's my mom
              lingering even longer
       bless her heart—

what can be dreamed from day turning to dark—
        soon its lights out for all of us—

    if you ask me to explain
I'm making   space

for flying through space   in words—

                        Is that enough, Mom?

Pink Suit

I saw my mother-in-law, Elsie
for the last time in March.
She handed me a pile
of sheets, apologetic
about the unmade guest bed.

So, it was cancer.
Doctors gave her six to twelve.
Hope they pass quickly.
She refused the treatments.
I am weary.

She led me to the guest room,
took the sheets,
waved a thin hand to motion
me out of the way.

Bottom sheet, top sheet,
blanket and coverlet, laid
each familiar layer in position.
She edged
carefully around each side,
stretched thin arms over
fabric with patterns faint
from washing.
Smoothed out ridges or lumps.

At the end,
folded back each corner,
to expose a splay of pastel triangles.

The many times she made up
these beds for her children. The worn
fabric silken with age.
By June she was gone.
At 94 buried

in her stylish pink suit,
black hair neat,
only a bit of gray.

I smooth my sheets, wish
her a mother's soft release.

Visiting Uncle Murray in the Senior Facility

You grasp my hand as if I were rescue.
      Too big too long sweat pants
keep falling down. One slipper,
one sneaker, we swing arms
down the dark hallway.
Out a back door to some
                resident-event
barbecue to watch a wigged
and made-up entertainer belt out
Frank Sinatra too loud
while you eat
        two plates of food
stare straight ahead.

I   replate   replay the bare bed in your
tiny room,   the metal chest with nothing inside
except a welcome brochure, coloring book.
      I had brought you gifts—a book, chocolates,
a wooden recorder, plus some photos of people
you should have known.
      You don't seem to. But you hold
the recorder like an old friend.

Why didn't you rescue him?
Kidnap him? Take him out
through the locked double doors?
      The alarm sounding frantic?
He would have loved it.

But I was about to say . . .

How could you let this happen?
This gentleman,
       a teacher, lover of children,
music maker and intrepid explorer,
         somehow became lost in the forest
of state regulations and guardianship.

Do you think this is an excuse?
No, but I suspect it's a limited metaphor.
I know Uncle Murray could have managed
a forest.
      No.   It's more like he somehow
merged onto the interstate by mistake.
      Imagine someone caught
              in a stream
of fast cars whizzing past,
      already a little confused at 93.
Say he exits around Jersey City,
    searches for home
in one shady neighborhood
             after another.

Somewhere along the route loses track of
      his wife
         his apartment with the grand piano and books.
       his personal rights.

    Instead ends up here
with only this black trash bag
mixed clean and dirty clothes—

no two shoes alike—shoved
into the bottom of a gray metal locker.
Bare mattress and pillow in plastic protectors.
The last we saw of him.

Do you really think you should be forgiven?
Look, I didn't see anyone else helping either.
        What can you expect?
One wrong turn after another—
cuss out a nurse? throw something?
                You could end up alone
curled into yourself
on a naked cot.

But, of course, you're right,
damned if I can forgive myself, either.

I can still see him holding the recorder
fingers poised over the holes
                        blowing gently.

Her Son

You enter the world, askew. You.
Bang your head on the concrete sidewalk.
You misfit this. Life. You. You bang your head.
Over and over again.

Adults think you odd, quirky, mental.
Kids call queer, weird, jerk. Something off.
Doesn't work. You fail at school. Can't
make friends, can't keep a job.
You depress, alone.

A surprise. For years you were not here.
Born in her fortieth year. We three grown.
This pregnancy lit her up. Your mother glowing.
Only DES kept it going. She. Lay in her bed
very quiet. Until the bleeding stopped.
Save the child.

Love hurts in the throat. She swallows
it all. The joy, the fear. Tentative pride.
Possible loss, salvation. Then, the birth of you,
the afterbirth like any bitch.
This life not. Over.

Your mother chews on these. Swallows,
digests. She's thinking of.
Still remembers. The quickening. Your pulse.
Baby words. Bright blond being.

You obsess over dead things. You fondle
a dead Bluefish, name it Lucy.

Pet her rough skin over and over. Worry
Grandmom will be cold in her grave.
Crippled birds? Can they fly
tossed out the upstairs window?

In your teens. I could use this word: deviant.
Your truck. Attacked with an ax. Set a fire
in the woods. Shot a cat, nailed
it to your closet wall.
Punched, kicked holes. Then holes.

It took twenty years to play out. All the way out.
All of them. Hard as concrete.
Each feels like hers. Slights. No friends. No job.
No single path forward. Each slight hers.

She absorbs the out of sync vibrations,
each deviation. Knows they are. Now say it.
(Her crying every day a clue) a premonition.
On a Sunday. You used your shotgun.

They buried you twenty feet from.
The family plot was where. Many years
later her blue coffin is lowered
into dirt. From there a wisp of her.
You.

A Small Paradigm Shift

My mother and I make a scrapbook to help her remember family. We paste pictures in perfect lines, place labels beneath each one. It's bad enough that memory leaves her—but faltering reason leaves the book to teeter on the bathroom windowsill, tumbles it into the bathtub. Whole structures start to dissolve. Bound pages, pictures, labels come unglued. Images shift, a few slide off altogether, flounder in the water. Others twist loose from their moorings like boats in a hurricane. As pictures fade family faces resemble the aged print of tiny flowers on the wallpaper in my old room. When dragged out, dried off, perspective has changed. Up and down transposed. Past inserts itself into present. Ocean depths layered atop bathers and beach umbrellas, girls in bikinis wear tilted top hats. A road stretching toward the horizon becomes a flare shooting at the sky. Whole families are beheaded by a child's birthday cake. Facts remain in flux as systems shift and settle. Panic is usual until the glue dries and meanings begin to coalesce. They can seem quite solid, for a time.

How to Build a Burger

My Dad the carpenter wore coveralls
carried a banged up black metal lunch box
to work. After church on Sundays he took us for rides.
We built that house. I did that garage.
See that big place over there? That's where
      I fell off the beam.

Friday nights after grocery shopping
our family ate a simple supper
of hamburger sandwiches. Dad
taught us how to build them.

First assemble the parts. Center
a slice of square white bread on a plate
and layer lettuce, onion, tomato. Then add
a greasy burger hot from the pan. Pile on pickles,
a smear of catsup, mayo or mustard—
never all three says dad—and top
with a square slice of American cheese.

The next part is tricky—requires some attention—
to engineer a bite that fits
between your teeth.   Squeeze the layers.   Open wide!
Invite the flavors to blend.   Juices stream
down your wrists.   Wait.
    What? Surely you can't have missed
this important cue—yes
You eat it with your hands!

Of course. You pick up the whole sandwich
and bite into a cross section. Lustily suck up
the juices, lick your fingers.

But then,
what would you think
if you took your Dad
to his favorite burger joint
ordered his usual mushroom burger
with fries and a pickle and watch
  as he stares   unfamiliar
    with the plate?   Then takes
his fork to the top of the bun,
toothpick still firmly impaling it,
    tears off a twist of dry bread,
then another.
               Methodically
        eats from the top down.

Watch the builder dismantle
his house.
                  Hear
the rattle of termites
chewing their way
up through the foundations.

Dementia Framed

I see Mother shoo them
together,
        smile-eyed
with adoration,
        to frame
all four generations.

Their faces
gaze from the square.

        What I see
     is the ghost of coveralls
  and the *stand up straight*
that's left of a father
head-shot and dizzy
        with dying.

In worn pink recliner
wearing a clean white shirt
     he sits   askew.
His   fear-battered black
lunch box
     off kilter,   lid
won't snap shut.
        The camera's
crack shows blue-gray eyes

   and a jawed clench
                          of terror,
     a fun-house mirror
of the baby's anxious
                     frown.

The child's father, and
                 grandfather,
wear absurd grins as if
     they were not kin
to great grandfather whose bellow
   is a strained whimper.

My eyes settle on his comb.
It stands upright
in his left shirt pocket,
      leftover
    from   an easier frame.

Cold

Rows of teddy bears, gingerbread men,
red and green hearts, stars, and gumdrops
decorate the white fleece blanket someone
gave my father years ago when he was dying.
Later, even in summer, Mom wrapped herself in it,
added the blue mittens I'd knit her,
cranked the heat up to eighty.

How I choked up to watch you wake
from surgery last year. You know,
when you were delirious with fever,
I brought it to keep you warm.
You barely knew I was there,
but latched onto that silly blanket like a raft
on cold white hospital linens.

I snap your picture with my phone
to remember the angles of bones,
the lines of nose, chin and shoulder.
Still hungry for what is between us,
surprised that my body at seventy-five
recalls the way it felt at sixteen—
steering quick through little creeks
in your boat, or at twenty, my arms
around your waist on the motorcycle,

the smell of salt water,
the pungent garlic you grow,
the briny taste of clams you open for me,
the color of the chambray shirts you've worn for years,
the same as your wisecrack blue eyes.

You are always cold now.
I pull tiny gingerbread men and snowmen
up around your shoulders, tuck
the death blanket around your edges,
sidle closer to your side.

A Manor of Endings

Next to the nurses' station
            in hell
you sat, my dapper, well-groomed
Dad in an adult diaper. When you
fell onto your face
        out of the wheelchair
they quietly replaced you.   I
   pretended   not to see.

Like a caged bird, your nails
had grown long   to curl
  in on themselves.
                No defense.
You could only rake your own skin
             —still alive.

When I tried
  to help you eat,
you pushed me   away,
       that forearm
          so strong,   a steady pressure.

You refused to   open
                        forgot how
to swallow. If a clever nurse
managed a spoon of applesauce
                past your lips,
            you held it there, in a puffed
cheek   indefinitely.

                After Medicare's allowed
twenty-one days you died.

One Woman's Breath

She ticked all the chores
off the list. Dance class,
volunteer work,
picked up mail, prescriptions,
stopped at last at the grocery store.

In the Piggly Wiggly parking lot
she sat in the air conditioning,
no groceries yet   just
to catch a breath. Perhaps
  an unfamiliar pain.

Her back canted
across the leather
head
       lolling
like a rag doll   on the glass.

Her husband gets the call.
       Now the space
she had stitched together
             begins to collapse.

Meanwhile
                lighter than breath
    she snatches up
        the dance costume
           the shopping lists
the obligations and expectations
              the sense of his touch
        the very air
              she once breathed
        scatters it all across the neighborhood
              like confetti.

Cuttings

I love how the tiny Geranium leaves pop from the dirt near the stem of the old leaf using its soft parts for nourishment before it withers. Something to rise up against.

She's a good girl, understands "no," you'd tell guests, then demonstrate my obedience with a command, a threat. Navy-trained, your brain a book of rules I don't understand. Why must we do chores on Saturday? Why can't we have friends over? Why do you blow up over every little thing? You chase me to the bathroom. I slam and lock the door while you yell about being barefoot outside with my boyfriend, though I know you're not mad about my feet. At my wedding you throw the boutonniere on the floor. And, yes, I am pregnant.

> I ate the candy
> from the forbidden dish, but
> don't wish you to wither.

My Brother Runs Down

His mother went alone to the marshes

                                           dropped her tears into

Phragmites and Cattails

Her youngest son

                                           She heard the ticks

Although the clock by his bedside had stopped

                                           She, paralyzed,

                                           the fuse sparking

Watched him run up, then down the stairs,

                                           I'm not going . . .

Then up again then

                                           a single shot

I don't know what happens when a bomb . . .

                                           But an eruption through him

That gun he'd got for hunting

                                           a twelfth birthday gift

Our lives blown out from its center

                                           I was not permitted to look

While police asked questions

                                          Young lieutenant paced the backyard

Fit savage kicks to a boy's bicycle

                                          I watched, wheels, ticking

Final Listening

I position myself on
the grave next door.
Bare trees bend in
cold March wind.

The sky is endless.
Fine. Clear. From here
life doesn't seem
quite so grim.

He was twenty. Swore he
wouldn't make twenty-one.
I shook it off, like a wet dog.

What else needed voice?
A single gunshot?
Bohemian Rhapsody
in his tape machine?

Perhaps my little brother
foresaw this one light—

how he might feel   safe
lying here.

For who can hurt
him now?

He is beyond.
        Below.

No Need

A dirty misshapen hat
battered coat on its hook
shavings of sawdust
on the bathroom rug

It is frigid
outside and the small fire
they made me is warm
              I sit in one
chair eat a dish of yogurt
someone hands me
                    I pile
the sink with single dishes maybe
someone else will wash
The sun highlights
streaks on the glass
but does not illumine the room

Last week I sat fully dressed
on top the bedclothes
all night Watched reruns
until I fell asleep exhausted
ready in case of need

There's no longer a need
though I keep opening the door
to peer out blankly

Aren't we always
caught unawares?

You could be stopped at the grocery
frying sausages or stumbling
to the bathroom at night

I'd done my best to prepare—
memorized every overused joke
familiar gesture
curve of muscle

I didn't plan on this desert
this parched throat of memory

V. Goodbye . . .

The Blinds Are Shut

It is dark inside her room, the smell
is dreadful. I look at her jammed shut eyes
head shaking side to side
for as long as I can stand, then scuttle
crab-like, bedside
then outside, then back
pulled by guilt
and fear and something
unspeakably—other—
about my mother.

Gulp fresh air, bird song
not sure what she is trying
              to not say
My own song   unformed
in my chest.

I hold her up over the plastic dishpan,
in that silly purple gown with the bright yellow
Tweety Bird she loved to wear,
wipe her broad forehead peppered
with wens and whorls, her mouth
with missing teeth. Stroke the long fingers,
missing the wedding ring she'd once again
                                misplaced.

Finally tuck her in.   *Maybe*
      if I stop fussing, you can sleep.
Kiss her. Go to bed.

Something about her closed eyes—

      made me play along—as if blind
to the escape she was making.

I could have sat vigil, helped
her through the night, perhaps
been there at the last breath,
      surely the test of a good daughter.

      But I was only partly brave
           partly good.

Dragging My Feet

I sat with you that last night.
        Comfort a gift
I kept trying
   to hand you.   But
          you shook me off   eyes closed.

In the morning I found you   left arm flung
over your head
       like a lazy stretch in bed
your face relaxed
              past pink   becoming wax.

My task to say—I'm the adult now—
  goodbye
    to call the officials
        inform the family.
And yet.

            And yet.

              I stood

at the foot of your bed.   Held
 your cold feet.
          Took
    the time.

The Tent Party

The elder now, I arrive early feeling oddly
responsible for the tent set up atop cold stones.
Tall men in dark suits pepper the scene, cluster
at tables already overflowing with flowers.

Now, an exaggeration of flowers cover my mother.
Silent, she commands attention from the pale
blue box. (She usually doesn't like parties)
They hand each guest a flower.

I had wanted pink rosebuds for her, but some snafu—
left only faded chrysanthemums. The rain
falls in spits and spurts, no kind of festive.
It is hard enough to stand, a mannequin

saying appropriate or inappropriate things.
Impossible to plan how to shape my face, my reflection
in the mirror a stranger. Now the rain is erasing
the makeup applied so carefully just an hour ago.

As if the tears hadn't done enough damage, rain
rolling down my cheeks, horizontal smears
from my arm erasing . . . hearty laughter
unfit for the occasion. We will give the flowers

to the kindly neighbor, the peace lily to a sad-looking
woman at Goodwill, who will agree to care for it.
Caring something Mom did well—
any lost dog, her pet parakeet, her children.

Then—people say things, including me,
and music is played. They cry,
say hello, goodbye. In black party dress
I stand first to lay my flower down.

I Just Want to See Her Face

Snowflakes fell like ashes wafting to earth
after a fire, the sky smoked gray. Driving home
        we flew down empty streets,
houses leaving me one after another.

Plain little homes in different colors
lined up close against the road. Where
families gathered to eat, play, sleep.

Black-green shrubs trimmed neat, lamppost
tied with Christmas wreath. The red bow, God!
the colors wormed their way inside.

One house painted a startled shade
of green on the side, the front.
Only after we'd passed saw
the far side was still
                a dirty peeling white.

Colored houses, the snow-covered
roads, snow falling wistful
        all driving me forward
                as I stretch backwards
        lest my love
is left behind
one side still unfinished.

Birdwing

She'd flown in the cool of darkness
her body vacant next morning.
Cold arms relaxed, face at peace
no sign of yesterday's torment.

Some officials came to take her away.
We surrendered her burial clothes.
They carried her past us, our outstretched
hands and silent tears in protest rose.
           Yet
we need not mourn. She wouldn't stay,
not linger there in some dark room
that creeps with sadness and the smell
of dust and dry decaying bloom.

She's loose in the woods, I know she is.
She wanders along some peaceful path.
Hums to herself a simple tune, touches
the trees as she moves past.
         Gone
to dirt and river and brush of leaf,
to air and breath on the wind,
to hollow and nest and tuft of feather,
part of song and birdwing.

VI. and now . . .

A Chance to Spring

April-soft rain on the window this morning like—

a quiet murmur that begs

I languish—
              just listen.

              My rocking chair the site
of delights—a coffee, warm buttered bread,
sweater and soft slippers, swaddled
in a blanket of rain light.

Things needing to be done. Shush! Here is
              a rainy excuse for meandering
among
                                  some
spent flowers,   sweet kisses—heady words.
Serious plans
      are for bright days.

After, I wander in secret places, mossy paths,
      see tiny violets hidden in grass.
              Winding
through fields
      I ponder tiny bluet and starflower.

              After violent shear of a mower,
punched-flat violet stems spring right back up.
                      I can't say that
I spring back up anymore

but simply   allow   the stem
    to rise
                    slowly
                        upright.

I Worry That My Grandchildren . . .

Picture me, when I get too old to chase you down.
    On stiff legs
           with frightful hair and missing teeth,
I totter out onto the front stoop,   waving,
   implore   one of you passing, *See*   *me.*

There are fairy tales about old women
                    living alone,
doors swinging open on their hinges,
        mice taking over the cupboards.

Years past, like the witch in the candy house, I lured
  young Hansels and Gretels   with cookies and cups of tea.
Now they are grown I stock five spice powder, zatar,
     and extra butter in case they run out.   My wicked price
conversation.   Even that is work, now, to suck up
    their fast-talking lingo through my
        thin straw.

Didn't her grandmother make Red Riding Hood's cape?
    The one she wore as she skipped
  carrying cake and wine   to her   sick
grandmother?
          Never mind about that wolf.
I have made   the capes and cakes.
   I want you
        to come skipping.

My own grandmother tried to crack a joke
    from that egg, (anguish).
         When no one

      had called her for a while, she'd telephone
our house
         Did you all break your arms?

But I wouldn't like to be the grandmother lying
in bed,   bedclothes up around my neck,
    just waiting
for girl   or wolf   or woodsman.
Better to
    get up,   shoulder my axe—
        my arm's not broken—
  and   hack away
      at that fable.

Best Behavior

When I think about it I am sometimes surprised at the quiet
devotion, the patience and tenderness we have toward each other
during the night, my husband and I, as we drop previously urgent
issues, concede important points, apologize for unkindness. As if
all of that is shallow, and what matters, now, is to lie side by side
and survive the long dark hours. Perhaps this is love.

But once I found crammed inside
a small wire rabbit cage,
our two Springer Spaniels. They'd trapped
themselves, and sat pressed together
quivering on their haunches.
A perfectly unmolested rabbit
sat shivering between them.
An existential fear in all
of their eyes. And all three noses
pointed straight at me.

Love at Seventy-Five

Is a lover's warm arm stretched around
a pillow. Silly but. The soft hairs. Then a plump
bottom lip and hot tongue. More than enough.
You want to nuzzle the rest of this body

of evidence of the past fifty years.
Time has where? Gone into little wrinkles
and patches of blood leaked beneath skin,
tiny lines inside folds of chin or cheek.

Bleak does not enter unseen. This body.
But you could decide not to play here.
Better to move along stout pathways
where nerves light up like lights

in the freezer section of the grocery
that turn on as you come near, saying *Stop here.
Open this door.* You want all of them.
No excuse for pouting and cringing when

you haven't yet been down the raspberry
crease in the elbow, the luscious melon of inner
thigh. Like at seventeen before you'd grasped
the extent of bodily terrain laid out for you.

Now at seventy-five playing catch-up
all the tricks of age up your sleeve
while you try to deceive the tired voice
still whining to just give up.

After the Death Certificate

1.

Having rounded up the deed to the house,
we set to work emptying
our childhood home.
At first we carefully sorted
then lost patience, began to toss
everything in the huge dumpster. Dozens
of tiny jars with screws of a particular size,
boxes of staples, buttons, labels,
ripped rugs thrown on rickety tables
a cascade of homemade VHS tapes
scattered between legs of the handsome
but unplayable piano. Then billows
of greeting cards, calendars, notepads
that came free in the mail rained
onto bits of ribbon, plastic containers.
Yet to-be-repaired vacuums and appliances
thrown on their heads, atop the hospital bed.
Over these fell shelves of Readers Digest
Condensed Books with stained dishcloths,
handmade afghans, blankets from past decades.
Bags of stretched brassieres and polyester pants
in awful assorted colors. All the pieces
of the stained bedroom carpet,
even the kitchen table.

2.

Imagine the giddiness
of being done,
at the mess you've just created
right in Dad's driveway
with him looking down.
Mom bemoaning the ruin
of some childhood memento
one of us made from macaroni.
Our whole life in trash.

3.

I've read of holy men
who possess only
a single bowl.
I'd add a large piece
of decent cloth
to drape around whatever place
needs it.
And let it be beautiful
in a hard-to-categorize color
a fabric with a good feel.
This
and my bowl for gruel.

                       Though
I suspect the dumpster
will gather me
in the end.

Generational

With polite laughter
you skim my surface
      while I admire your bright skin, shine
of hair and slim young thoughts.

I remember well
the string of lies
you will need to tell yourself
as March lures the bud of daffodil
  through frozen soil   into cold snow.

Shine your light
over my generalities. You deserve more
      but can't imagine it yet.

You will find here your own reflection
     cast in my eyes' mirror.
Go ahead,   hold me off
while you crack the shell
of your life.   I'm still engaged
  but wallow in deeper pools
murky,   where regret attaches
        —like parasites on aged skin

When you are old as I am
what will you dig out
   of what is left?

In the cleft   between energy
and matter there still works
the germ of life. Will
you remember

        how fierce
I loved you? Let it stir you?

What will remain
of this face
        these tears?
For years
    I pore myself
over your meaning.

To Change Direction

Our Beech trees are diseased, their leaves cracked with black, they drop while still green.
It is easy to imagine danger in places I can't see.

Fall limps toward us, late and bedraggled.
When I retire I will use my old sewing machine again, feed a sourdough starter, pick up abandoned knitting.

Picnics with my mother, lying on a blanket we made stories from the clouds.
It is hard to wait for the next thing.

In the breeze, trees squeak and creak like rusted scissors, cut the sky into blue squares.
I linger over what is left behind.

The bones of the trees are sturdy though their bark is flocked with scale. When these trees die, our forest will transform.
I remember the way my mother smoothed my forehead, *it will be alright.*

Milkweed spills out of its pods. White feathery piles litter the ground.
I wonder when the wind will set summer free.

Three brown cows calmly graze the field.
I hesitate to become a stranger.

Amid the trees thousands of winged maple keys are picked up by
 the wind.
Will there be enough? I am hopeful.

My husband's bones are sturdy and his hands warm.
I pay attention.

Finally a breeze comes up and the milkweed flies, like soap
 bubbles flung across the field with a plastic wand.
Spinning.

Months before her death, my mother and I clasp hands.
I recall her hands' coolness, the length of her fingers.

Pileated woodpeckers have made three huge holes in a dead tree.
 Our urgent grip on the familiar.

The fields are full of final things—seed pods, weeds, skeletons of
 Queen Anne's Lace.
I wonder who will sing my name?

About the Author

Jean Anne Feldeisen lives with her husband of more than fifty years on a farm in Maine. She is a retired psychotherapist, a grandmother, and a writer.

For her seventieth birthday, Jean self-published a memoir, *Dear Milly*. She has written essays for *Next Avenue, Chicken Soup for the Soul,* and *The Dirty Spoon*. Jean has been a host for the *Crows Feet: Life as We Age Podcast* since 2022. Her poetry has been published in *The Orchards Poetry Journal, Rising Phoenix Review, Vita Poetica, Neologism, The Eunoia Review, The Raven's Perch, Bracken, The Hopper,* and *Spank the Carp,* among other publications and anthologies.

Her first poetry chapbook, *Not All Are Weeping,* was released in May of 2023 by Main Street Rag Publishing Company. In September of 2023, she and her friend, Argy Nestor, self-published their collection of poetry and images, *Catching Fireflies*. Jean is crazy about knitting, yoga, playing classical piano, and making special meals for her family.

Follow her at:
jeanfeldeisen.com

www.ingramcontent.com/pod-product-compliance
Lightning Source LLC
Chambersburg PA
CBHW072157160426
43197CB00012B/2426